alogue

To my father and mother

Published by William Collins Sons and Co Ltd
First Published 1976
Latest reprint 1977
Copyright © Woman magazine 1976
Printed in Great Britain

ISBN 0 00 410325 4

CAT-alogue

Bruce Angrave

Collins Glasgow and London

Im-puss-ible

S-purr-s

50 puss-ent

Puss-t Impressionist

Cup-purr

Table claw-th

Octo-puss

Do-it-yourself kit

Paw-tly

Su-purr-stition

Purr-jamas

Puss-ionate

Mew-sic

Purr-haps

Kit-bag

Purr-m

Mephisto-fur-les

Mew-tation

Purr-pendicular

Paw-celain

Puss-terity

Purr-achutist

Hy-purr-chondriac

Cor-puss-cles

De-mew-re

Purr-cussion

Preci-puss

Paw-table

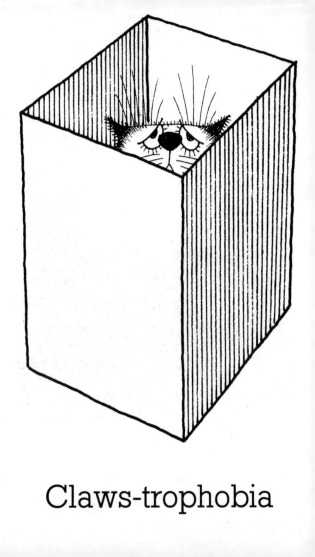

Claws-trophobia

Purr-spiration

Fur-mented

As-purr-in

Im-puss-onator

Puss-essive

Im-purr-vious

Tres-puss-er

Puss-t graduate

Im-purr-tinent

Philanthro-puss-t

ISHMONGER

Purr-loin

One Plain one Purr-l

Chea-purr

Purr-itan

Paw-nography

Paw-trait

Puss-illanimous

Purr-fume

S-kit-tle

Su-purr-market

Purr-nickety

Puss-imist

Identi-kit

Purr-colator

Purr-forated

Paw-puss

Mog-netic

Combus-tibble

Gr-rr-rr-rr-rr

Survival-kit

Mantel-puss

Santa-Claws

Puss-terior